WHAT'S INSIDE?

Discover more about the world of extreme animals!

Cheetahs

Chameleons

Frogs

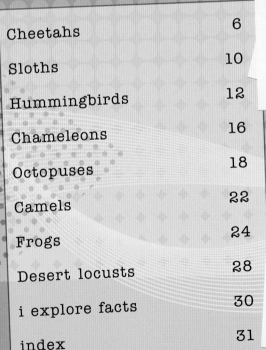

Sloths

Hummingbirds

Octopuses

Camels

Desert locusts

i explore facts

CHEETAHS

Class: Mammals

Using their long legs, cheetahs can run at up to 62 mph (100 kph) over a short distance! They don't need long to catch their targets though – a typical chase is over in 20 seconds.

leg

i discover

Strong legs and hard paws help a cheetah fly over the ground with strides that are 23 ft (7 m) long – that's longer than a car! A long tail also allows it to change direction during a chase.

paw

Cheetah's tear lines

Scientists think a cheetah's tear lines protect its eyes from the glare of bright sunlight. This helps it see prey more clearly.

tail

Cheetah sprinting

i learn

When a cheetah sprints, all four of its feet can lift off the ground at the same time – as if it is flying through the air!

spotted coat

i fact

Cheetahs are stealthy hunters. Their spotted coats allow them to blend in to the long grass without being seen.

SLOTHS

Class: Mammals

Sloths are the slowest mammals in the world! They spend most of their lives hanging upside down in tropical forests.

Sloth sleeping

i fact

Sloths are not as lazy as people think! They actually only sleep for about 10 hours a day.

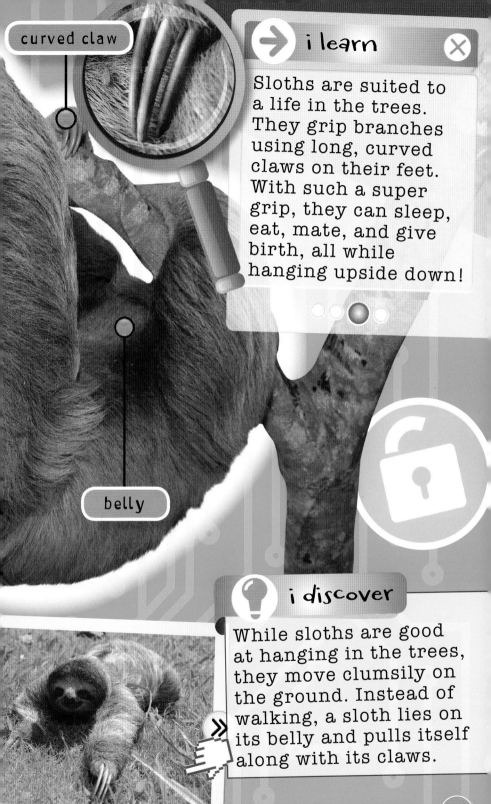

curved claw

i learn

Sloths are suited to a life in the trees. They grip branches using long, curved claws on their feet. With such a super grip, they can sleep, eat, mate, and give birth, all while hanging upside down!

belly

i discover

While sloths are good at hanging in the trees, they move clumsily on the ground. Instead of walking, a sloth lies on its belly and pulls itself along with its claws.

Sloth on the ground

11

HUMMINGBIRDS

Class: Birds

By beating their small wings incredibly fast, beautiful hummingbirds can hover expertly in the air. Hummingbirds are skilled fliers and can move forward, backward, sideways, and even fly upside down!

beak

Hummingbird feeding

12

Hummingbirds are named after the humming sound their wings make when they hover at high speeds. While they are excellent at flying, they are not very good at walking or hopping because their legs are very short!

wing

Rufous-tailed hummingbird sitting in a nest ⊗

leg

i facts

Hummingbirds build the smallest nests of any bird. The vervain hummingbird's nest is the size of half a walnut shell.

The bee hummingbird is only 2¼ in (57 mm) long, which is smaller than some butterflies!

 i discover

Hummingbirds need to eat a lot of food to fuel their acrobatic flying. They feed on nectar from flowers by sticking out their long tongues while hovering in the air.

CHAMELEONS

Class: Reptiles

Amazing chameleons are famous for their ability to change color. Some do this to blend in to their surroundings, but most change color to show other chameleons what they are feeling.

i discover

Using their long, sticky tongues, chameleons feed mainly on insects. They shoot out their tongues quickly to catch their prey before it escapes!

Chameleon catching its prey

tail

Chameleons are able to look at two things at once! They can move their eyes in different directions at the same time. This gives them a 360-degree view of the world around them.

eye

skin

toes

Pygmy stump-tailed chameleon

Tiny dwarf chameleons can look just like dead leaves! If threatened, they will drop to the leaf-covered ground and lie very still.

OCTOPUSES

Class: Cephalopods

Eight-armed octopuses are smart sea creatures. They can squeeze their bodies into tight and tiny spaces to hide from predators.

Octopus hiding

 i fact

j To escape an attack, an octopus can lose an arm and then regrow it afterwards!

 i learn

An octopus's arms are covered in strong suckers. It uses its suckers to hold things and grip its prey tightly.

sucker

arm

i discover

Like most octopuses, the mimic octopus can change its color and patterns to blend in. Amazingly, it can also change shape to look like other animals such as sea snakes or flatfish.

imic octopus

The blue-ringed octopus is very dangerous. It is venomous enough to kill a person.

Blue-ringed octopus

CAMELS

Class: Mammals

Bactrian camel

Camels live in extreme environments!
By storing fat in their humps, they
can survive several weeks in
the desert without food.

Dromedary camels

i fact

Dromedary camels have one
hump, and Bactrian camels
have two. Camels that have
not eaten for a long time
may not have a hump at all!

mel resting in the desert

Camels can last several months without water – even when it is extremely hot. To save even more water, a camel doesn't sweat until its body temperature hits 105°F (40.5°C)!

hump

mouth

eyelashes

i learn

Camels are suited to life in the sandy desert. They can use their long, thick eyelashes to keep out grains of sand, and they have tough mouths for eating thorny plants.

FROGS

Class: Amphibians

Frogs live and breathe on land and in water! On land, a frog can breathe using its lungs, but in water, it takes in oxygen through its skin.

head

belly

i learn

The bright color of the tiny golden poison dart frog warns others to stay away from its poisonous skin! It's the most poisonous frog in the world and although it only grows to 1.5 in (3.5 cm), it could kill ten grown men with its poison.

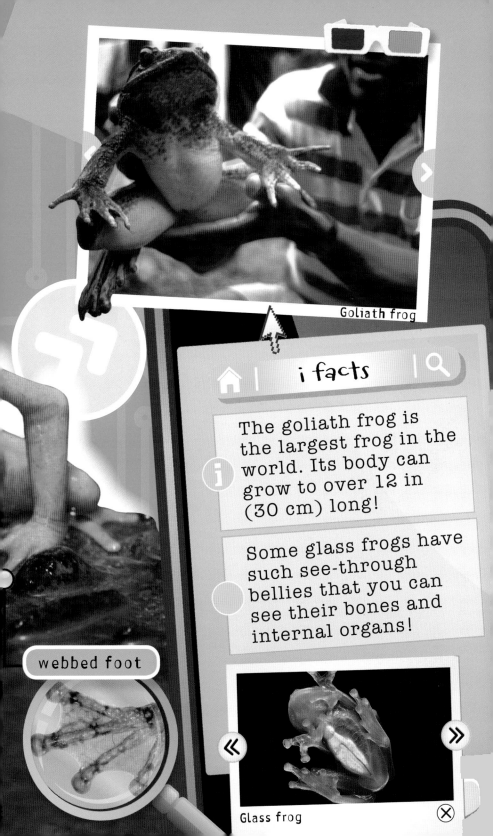

Goliath frog

i facts

The goliath frog is the largest frog in the world. Its body can grow to over 12 in (30 cm) long!

Some glass frogs have such see-through bellies that you can see their bones and internal organs!

webbed foot

Glass frog

i discover

The Wallace's flying tree frog appears to fly between the trees! It jumps, then spreads out its four webbed feet like a parachute to glide through the air. Sticky pads on its feet help it land softly and stick to the trees.

DESERT LOCUSTS

Class: Insects

Desert locusts are the world's most destructive insects! When rain is plentiful, and there are more plants to eat, they reproduce rapidly.

ℹ In just one day, a small swarm of 50 million locusts can eat enough food to feed 400 people for a year.

Locust eating

Adult desert locusts can travel enormous distances. One swarm flew from West Africa to the Caribbean!

Flying locust ✕

eye

leg

wing

✕

i learn

Locusts form huge groups called swarms. These swarms can combine to form a giant swarm that can stretch up to 40 miles (60 km) wide. The swarm eats all the crops in its path and can cause people to starve.

i explore FACTS

An easy way to remember the difference between the Dromedary and Bactrian camels is to take the first letter of each name and turn it on its side: D means one hump and B means two!

The largest land animal is the African elephant, but the largest animal in the world is the blue whale.

Sharks have a super sense of smell – it is said that they can even smell another fish's fear!

The ostrich has the largest eye of any land animal. Its eye is eight times the size of a human eye!

The world record-holder for the most number of legs is a millipede that had 375 pairs of legs!

Giraffes are the tallest animals in the world. At over 20 in (50 cm) long, even their tongues are enormous!